Pierre Rode
1774 – 1830

24 Caprices
24 Capricen

in form of Etudes for Violin alone, in all 24 Keys
in Etüdenform für Violine allein, in allen 24 Tonarten
en forme d'Etudes pour Violon seul, dans les 24 Ton

Edited with Preparatory Exercises
Revidiert und mit Vorübungen versehen
Editées avec exercices préparatoires et variantes

by / von / de
Max Rostal

ED 6512
ISMN 979-0-001-06920-5

www.schott-music.com

Mainz · London · Berlin · Madrid · New York · Paris · Prague · Tokyo · Toronto
© 1974/2008 SCHOTT MUSIC GmbH & Co. KG, Mainz · Printed in Germany

VORWORT

Der französische Geiger und Komponist Jacques Pierre Joseph Rode wurde am 16. Februar 1774 in Bordeaux geboren und starb am 26. November 1830 in Château de Bourbon bei Damazon (Lot-et-Garonne). Im Jahre 1787 wurde er Schüler von Viotti in Paris, der ihn 1790 im „Théatre de Monsieur" mit einem seiner eigenen Violinkonzerte der Öffentlichkeit vorstellte. Rode wurde dann als Führer der zweiten Geigen im „Théâtre Feydeau" angestellt und später wurde er als Soloviolinist an die Opera berufen, wo er bis 1799 blieb. Schon während dieser Zeit ab 1794 konzertierte er mit Garat in Hamburg, Berlin, Holland und England und wurde 1795 Professor am „Conservatoire". 1799 reiste Rode nach Spanien, wo er mit dem berühmten Cellisten und Komponisten Boccherini zusammentraf. Mit Boieldieu ging er 1803 nach St. Petersburg und wurde Soloviolinist beim Zar Alexander I. mit einem Gehalt von 5000 Rubel. 1808 - 11 lebte er wieder in Paris, aber sein Erfolg war wesentlich geringer als in früheren Zeiten. Spohr hörte Rode ursprünglich bei dessen Durchreise in Braunschweig und war erstmals so beeindruckt, daß er für eine geraume Zeit versuchte Rode's Stil zu imitieren. Jedoch später (im Jahre 1813) hörte Spohr ihn wieder in Wien und berichtet in seiner Autobiographie von seiner Enttäuschung über das Spiel von Rode, welches er maniriert und ungenügend im Technischen wie auch im Stil fand. Bei weiteren Konzertreisen traf Rode in Wien auch Beethoven, der ausdrücklich für Rode seine wundervolle Sonate in G Dur op. 96 schrieb, die von Erzherzog Rudolph und Rode bei einem Privatkonzert aufgeführt wurde. Beethoven war allerdings mit der Interpretation Rode's nicht zufrieden, und bald danach bat er den Erzherzog, den Geigenpart an Rode zu senden, damit dieser vor einer zweiten Aufführung das Werk sich genauer ansieht. Mendelssohn berichtet im April 1825, daß Rode durch diese Begebenheit und seinen generellen Mißerfolg den festen Entschluß faßte, nie wieder eine Geige in die Hand zu nehmen. Diese Enttäuschungen nahm sich Rode so zu Herzen, daß sich fortan seine Gesundheit zunehmned verschlechterte.

Rode's Kompositionen sind bis heute bei den Geigern sehr beliebt, und seine Violinkonzerte und vor allem die vorliegenden „24 Caprices en forme d'études dans les 24 tons de la gamme" sind nach wie vor bei jedem Geiger unerläßlich. Die Capricen werden immer ihren Platz neben denen von Kreutzer, Dont, Wieniawski und Paganini behalten, da sie von größtem Wert für eine solide Ausbildung auf der Geige sind. Aber auch die Anwendung von Rode's Capricen auf der Bratsche hat sich als äußerst nützlich erwiesen.

Max Rostal

PRÉFACE

Né le 16 février 1774 à Bordeaux, le violoniste et compositeur français Jacques Pierre Joseph Rode mourut le 26 novembre 1830 au château de Bourbon près de Damazon (Lot-et-Garonne). En 1787 il devint, à Paris, l'élève de Viotti qui le présenta en public trois ans plus tard, au Théâtre de Monsieur, dans l'un de ses propres concertos pour violon. Rode fut ensuite engagé comme chef des seconds violons au Théâtre Feydeau, puis comme violon solo à l'Opéra, où il demeura jusqu'en 1799. Dès cette époque, il entreprit avec Garat, à partir de 1794, des tournées de concerts qui le conduisirent à Hambourg, à Berlin, en Hollande et en Angleterre et fut nommé professeur au Conservatoire en 1795. En 1799 Rode fit un voyage en Espagne, où il rencontra le fameux violoncelliste et compositeur Boccherini. En 1803 il partit avec Boieldieu pour Saint-Pétersbourg, où le tsar Alexandre Ier l'engagea comme violon solo aux appointements de 5000 roubles. Entre 1808 et 1811 il vécut à nouveau à Paris, mais sans y retrouver, a beaucoup près, ses succès passés. Spohr entendit d'abord Rode lors du passage de ce dernier à Brunswick et cette première rencontre l'impressionna si fortement que, pendant un certain temps, il n'eut d'autre ambition que d'imiter le style de Rode. Plus tard cependant (en 1813), il l'entendit à nouveau à Vienne et son autobiographie rapporte la déception que lui causa le jeu de Rode, qu'il trouva maniéré et défectueux à la fois techniquement et sur le plan stylistique. Au cours d'autres tournées, Rode rencontra également a Vienne Beethoven et ce dernier écrivit expressément pour lui sa merveilleuse sonate en sol majeur op. 96, que l'archiduc Rodolphe et Rode jouèrent lors d'un concert privé. Beethoven, il est vrai, ne fut pas satisfait de l'interprétation de Rode et, peu après, il demanda a l'archiduc d'envoyer la partie de violon à celui-ci afin qu'il l'étudiât de plus près avant une seconde exécution. Mendelssohn rapporte en avril 1825 la ferme résolution prise par Rode, à la suite de cet incident et de son insuccès généralisé, de ne plus jamais toucher à un violon. Ces déceptions affectèrent Rode à un tel point que, désormais, sa santé en fut de plus en plus ébranlée.

Aujourd'hui encore, les compositions de Rode sont fort appréciées des violonistes: ses concertos et surtout les «24 Caprices en forme d'études dans les 24 tons de la gamme» qui font l'objet de la présente publication demeurent indispensables à quiconque est soucieux d'acquérir une parfaite maîtrise de l'instrument. Les Caprices, notamment, conserveront toujours leur place à côté de ceux de Kreutzer, de Dont, de Wieniawski et de Paganini. Leur étude s'est en outre révélée des plus utiles également aux altistes.

Max Rostal

PREFACE

The French violinist and composer Jacques Pierre Joseph Rode was born on February 16th, 1774 in Bordeaux and died on November 26th, 1830 in Château de Bourbon near Damazon (Lot-et-Garonne). He became a pupil of Viotti 1787 in Paris, who introduced him to the public in 1790 at the "Théatre de Monsieur" with one of his own violinconcertos. Rode was afterwards engaged as the leader of the second violins at the "Théatre Feydeau" and later became Soloviolinist at the Opera, where he stayed until 1799. During this time (since 1794) he gave concerts with Garat in Hamburg, Berlin, Holland and England and was appointed Professor at he "Conservatoire" in 1795. Rode travelled 1799 to Spain, where he met the celebrated cellist and composer Boccherini. With Boieldieu he went to St. Petersburg in 1803 and became Soloviolinist to Alexander I. with a salary of 5000 Rubels. From 1808 to 1811 he lived again in Paris, but his success diminished considerably, compared with previous triumphs. Spohr heard Rode for the first time at a concert in Brunswick and was so impressed, that he tried to copy Rode's style for a lengthy period, but later on (in 1813) Spohr listened again to Rode in Vienna and reports in his Autobiography about his disappointment of Rode's playing, which he now found mannered and technically, as well as stylistically far below Rode's original powers.On a further concert-tour, Rode met also Beethoven in Vienna, who wrote the wonderful Sonata in G major, op. 96 specifically for him and which was performed by the Archduke Rudolph and Rode at a private concert. Beethoven was not very happy with Rode's interpretation of the violin-part and soon afterwards asked the Archduke to send the music to Rode, so that he could look at the work more closely before a second performance. Mendelssohn reported in April 1825, that Rode made a firm decision never to touch a fiddle again, after his many disappointments and failure to regain his former success. This he took so much to heart, that his health deteriorated rapidly.

Rode's compositions are generally liked by violinists even up to now and his violinconcerti and particularly his "24 Caprices en forme d'études dans les 24 tons de la gamme" are still standard-works of every violinist. The Caprices will always keep their place along those of Kreutzer, Dont, Wieniawski and Paganini, as they remain essential and of the greatest value for a sound education on the violin. But also the application of these Caprices on the Viola has proved to be most useful and of great value.

Max Rostal

Zeichenerklärung

⊓	Herunterstrich
V	Heraufstrich
⟅══════⟆	Ganzer Bogen
⟅═══|	Obere Hälfte des Bogens
|═══⟆	Untere Hälfte des Bogens
⟅═	Spitze des Bogens
≥	Mitte des Bogens
⟆	Am Frosch des Bogens
⎯	Lange Note, doch etwas abgesetzt
•	Kurze Note auf der Saite (Martelé)
⎯•⎯	Kurze Note auf der Saite, jedoch länger als . ohne —
▾	Kurze Note springend (Spiccato oder Sautillé)
⎯▼⎯	Kurze Note springend, jedoch länger als ▾ ohne —
⌒•	Punkt außerhalb des Bindebogens bedeutet Verkürzung dieser Note, ohne vorherige Luftpause
⌒▾ oder ⌒•	Punkt innerhalb des Bindebogens bedeutet Luftpause vor der Note, im ersten Fall durch Bogenhebung und im zweiten auf der Saite
[	Akkorde ohne Brechung
↑	Akkorde ohne Brechung und oben durchgehalten
↓	Akkorde ohne Brechung und unten durchgehalten
⦚	Arpeggio
⦚↑	Arpeggio aufwärts
⦚↓	Arpeggio abwärts
I	E - Saite
II	A - Saite
III	D - Saite
IV	G - Saite
⌐⎯	Finger liegen lassen
⊐	Stummes Aufsetzen des Fingers
restez	In der Lage bleiben
≣	Kleine Note ohne Hals ist kein Vorschlag, sondern ein Hinweis, daß der Triller mit der oberen Note beginnt

Fingersätze und Bogenstriche zwischen Klammern sind alternative Vorschläge

Metronom-Bezeichnungen sind nur approximativ aufzufassen und sind als Höchstgrenze der Geschwindigkeit gedacht. Anfänglich soll alles langsam geübt werden und dementsprechend sind Bogenteilungen vorzunehmen.

Explication des signes utilisés

⊓	Tirez
V	Poussez
⊏══════⊓	Avec toute la longueur de l'archet
⊏══|	Avec la moitié supérieure de l'archet
|══⊓	Avec la moitié inférieure de l'archet
⊏═	Avec la pointe de l'archet
══	Avec le milieu de l'archet
⊏⊓	Avec le talon de l'archet
—	Note longue, mais légèrement détachée
•	Note brève sur la corde (Martelé)
⊤•	Note brève sur la corde, mais plus longue que . sans —
▾	Note brève, spiccato ou sautillé
⊤▾	Note brève, sautillé, mais plus longue que ▾ sans —
⌢•	Le point en dehors de la liaison signifie que la note correspondante doit être abrégée, mais sans être précédée d'aucune respiration
⌢▾ ou ⌢•	Le point à l'intérieur de la liaison indique une respiration avant la note, dans le premier cas en levant l'archet, dans le second sur la corde
[	Accords non brisés
↑	Accords non brisés et tenus en haut
↓	Accords non brisés et tenus en bas
⦚	Arpège
⦚	Arpège ascendant
⦚	Arpège descendant
I	Corde de *mi*
II	Corde de *la*
III	Corde de *ré*
IV	Corde de *sol*
⌐⌐	Laisser le doigt sur la corde
⌐	Pose muette du doigt
restez	Conserver la même position
𝄞	Une petite note sans queue n'est pas une appoggiature mais elle indique que le trille commence à la note supérieure.

Les indications de doigté et de coups d'archet entre crochets sont suggérées
à titre de variantes.

Les indications métronomiques n'ont qu'une valeur approximative et elles
constituent en tout cas une limite maxima pour la vitesse. Au début, il convient de
tout travailler lentement en utilisant les sections appropriées de l'archet.

Explanation of signs

⊓	Down bow
V	Up bow
▭▭▭⊓	Whole bow
▭=|	Upper half of bow
|═⊓	Lower half of bow
▭	Tip of bow
══	Middle of bow
⊓	Heel (or Frog) of bow
—	Long note, but slightly detached
•	Short note on the string (Martelé)
⊤•	Short note on the string, but longer than . without —
▾	Short note off the string (Spiccato or Sautillé)
⊤▾	Short note off the string, but longer than ▾ without —
⌢•	Dot outside slur means shortening of that particular note, without stopping before it.
⌢▾ or ⌢•	Dot inside slur means stopping before that note, in the first instance by lifting the bow, in the second by leaving the bow on the string
[	Chords without spreading
↑	Chords without spreading and sustaining top notes
↓	Chords without spreading and sustaining bottom notes
⌇	Arpeggio
↿	Arpeggio upwards
⇂	Arpeggio downwards
I	E - String
II	A - String
III	D - String
IV	G - String
⌐⎯⌐	Keep finger on the string
⊐	Silent stopping of finger
restez	Stay in position
(small note)	Small note without stem is not a grace-note, but an indication that the Trill starts with the upper auxiliary note

Fingerings and bowings between brackets are alternative suggestions

Metronom-Markings are only approximate and represent the upper limit of speed. Everything should be practised slowly to start with and the bowings have to be divided accordingly.

10

2. *Allegretto* (♩. = 92)

A-Moll
A-minor
La-mineur

3.

G-Dur
G-major
Sol-majeur

Comodo (♩ = 120)

20

a) Alles auf der G-Saite bis ★
   All on the G-String until ★
   Tout sur la corde de sol jusqu'a ★

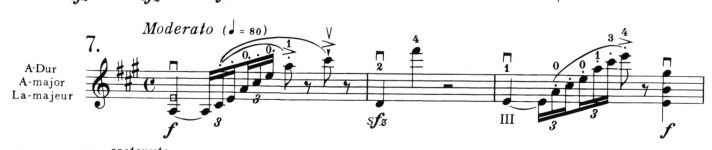

7.

A-Dur
A-major
La-majeur

Moderato (♩ = 80)

24

8.

Fis-Moll
F#-minor
Fa#-mineur

Moderato assai (♩.=84)

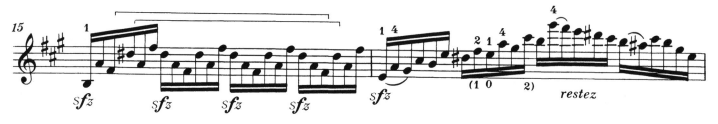

9.

Adagio (♪ = 69)

E-Dur
E-major
Mi-majeur

10.

Cis-Moll
C#-minor
Ut#-mineur

Allegretto (♩. = 76)

Edition Schott

Pierre Rode

1774 – 1830

24 Caprices

24 Capricen

Preparatory Exercises and Variations
Übungsvorschläge und Varianten
Exercices préparatoires et variantes

ED 6512
ISMN 979-0-001-06920-5

SCHOTT

www.schott-music.com

Mainz · London · Berlin · Madrid · New York · Paris · Prague · Tokyo · Toronto
© 1974/2008 SCHOTT MUSIC GmbH & Co. KG, Mainz · Printed in Germany

Caprice 1

Caprice 2

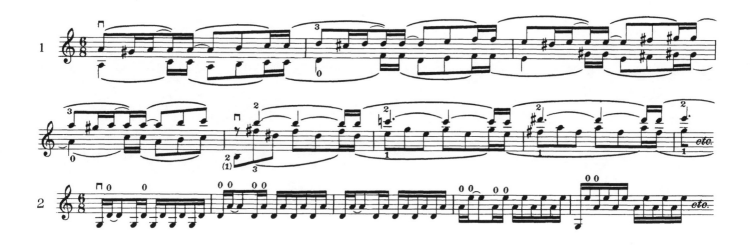

Caprice 3

2 — Die Übungen 2.-3. und 4. auch mit V anfangen, also umgekehrt.

3 — Commencer aussi les exercises 2.-3. et 4. par V, puis inversement.

4 — The exercises 2.-3. and 4. also with V starting, therefore reversed.

Caprice 4

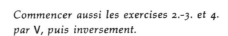

Takt 19 - 20   Mesure 19 - 20   Bar 19 - 20

Die ganze Caprice vom Allegro im De-taché, dann aber auch im Sautillé.

Tout ce Caprice à partir de l'Allegro en détaché, puis aussi en sautillé.

The entire Caprice from the Allegro in Detaché, but then also in Sautillé.

Caprice 5

Takt 37 - 39   Mesure 37 - 39   Bar 37 - 39

Takt 64 - 67   Mesure 64 - 67   Bar 64 - 67

Caprice 6

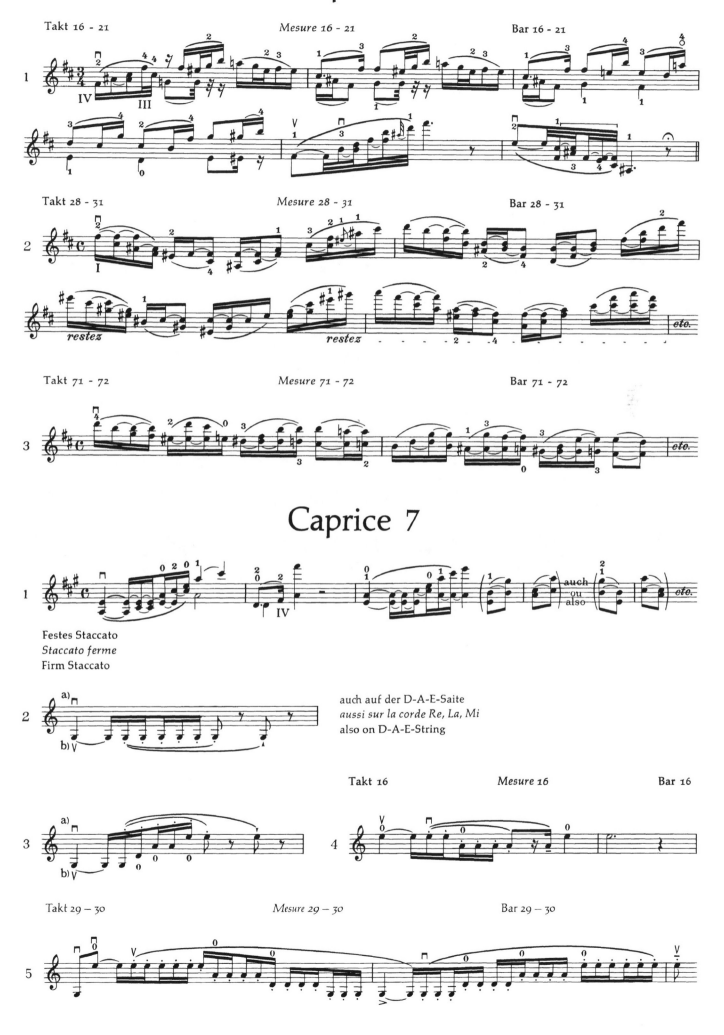

Takt 16 - 21   Mesure 16 - 21   Bar 16 - 21

Takt 28 - 31   Mesure 28 - 31   Bar 28 - 31

Takt 71 - 72   Mesure 71 - 72   Bar 71 - 72

Caprice 7

Festes Staccato
Staccato ferme
Firm Staccato

auch auf der D-A-E-Saite
aussi sur la corde Re, La, Mi
also on D-A-E-String

Takt 16   Mesure 16   Bar 16

Takt 29 – 30   Mesure 29 – 30   Bar 29 – 30

6

Caprice 8

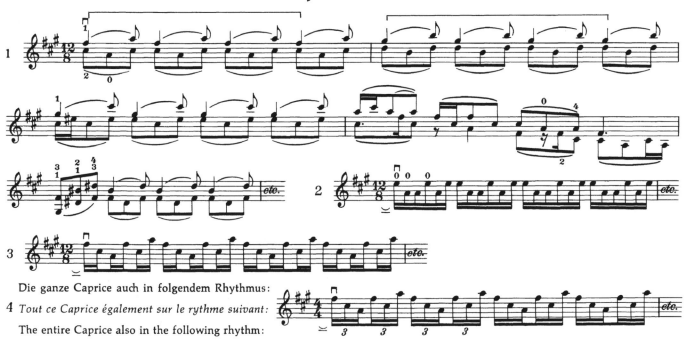

Im Detaché, aber auch im Sautillé zu üben.

A travailler en détaché, mais aussi en sautillé.

To be practised in Detaché, but also in Sautillé.

Caprice 9

Das Allegretto ist vom Komponisten durchwegs in der vierten Lage konzipiert.

L'Allegretto est entièrement conçu en quatrième position par le compositeur.

The Allegretto is conceived entirely in the fourth position by the composer.

Das Allegretto im Detaché, aber auch im Spiccato.

L'Allegretto en détaché, mais aussi en spiccato.

The Allegretto in Detaché, but also in Spiccato.

Caprice 10

Diese Caprice ist vom Komponisten durchwegs in der dritten Lage konzipiert.

Ce Caprice est entièrement conçu en troisième position par le compositeur.

This Caprice is conceived entirely in the third position by the composer.

Die ganze Caprice auch in folgendem Rhythmus:

4 *Tout ce Caprice également sur le rythme suivant:*

The entire Caprice also in the following rhythm:

Im Detaché, aber auch in Sautillé.   *En détaché, mais aussi en sautillé.*   In Detaché, but also in Sautillé.

Caprice 11

Takt 5 - 8   *Mesure 5 - 8*   Bar 5 - 8

Takt 23 - 28   *Mesure 23 - 28*   Bar 23 - 28

Takt 78 - 80   *Mesure 78 - 80*   Bar 78 - 80

Caprice 12

Die ganze Caprice auch in folgendem Rhythmus:

3 *Tout ce Caprice également sur le rythme suivant:*

The entire Caprice also in the following rhythm:

8

Caprice 13

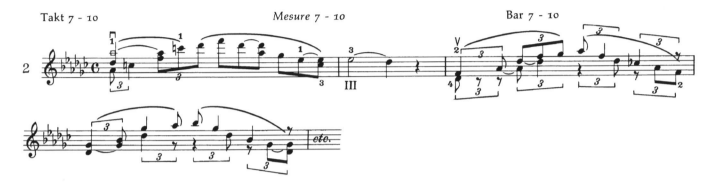

Caprice 14

Caprice 15

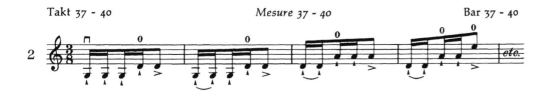

Takt 37 - 40 — **Mesure 37 - 40** — **Bar 37 - 40**

Caprice 16

Die ganze Caprice zuerst ohne Triller üben.

Travailler d'abord tout ce Caprice sans trilles.

The entire Caprice to be practised at first without trills.

Takt 8 - 9 — **Mesure 8 - 9** — **Bar 8 - 9**

Caprice 17

Auf Klangreinheit und rhythmische Ebenmäßigkeit besonders achten.

Veiller particulièrement à la pureté du son et à l'égalité rythmique.

Purity of sound and rhythmical evenness to be observed particularly.

Takt 15 - 27 — **Mesure 15 - 27** — **Bar 15 - 27**

Caprice 18

Takt 9 - 14 — **Mesure 9 - 14** — **Bar 9 - 14**

Caprice 19

Takt 51 - 54   Mesure 51 - 54   Bar 51 - 54

Caprice 20

Takt 9 - 12   Mesure 9 - 12   Bar 9 - 12

Takt 17 - 19   Mesure 17 - 19   Bar 17 - 19

Takt 31 - 32   Mesure 31 - 32   Bar 31 - 32

Caprice 21

Caprice 22

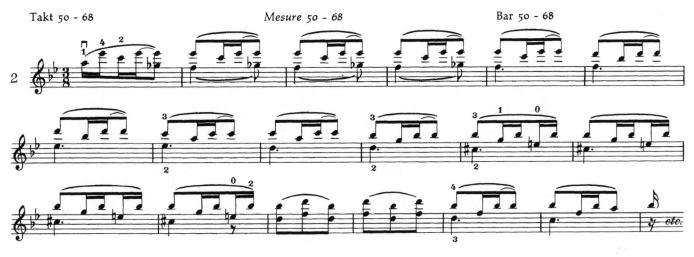

Takt 50 - 68   *Mesure 50 - 68*   Bar 50 - 68

Takt 88 - 100   *Mesure 88 - 100*   Bar 88 - 100

Caprice 23

12

5

6 Alle Vorübungen auch für Takt 8 - 10 anwenden.

Appliquer également aux mesures 8 - 10 tous les exercices préparatoires.

All preparatory exercises to be applied to bar 8 - 10.

Takt 17 - 20 *Mesure 17 - 20* **Bar 17 - 20**

7

Takt 26 - 29 *Mesure 26 - 29* **Bar 26 - 29**

8

Caprice 24

Takt 4 - 8 *Mesure 4 - 8* **Bar 4 - 8**

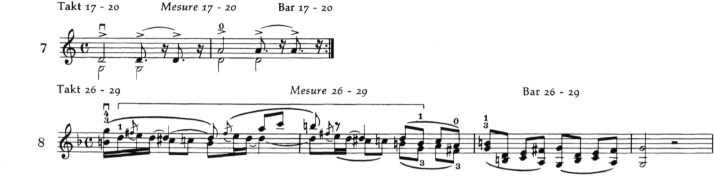

Takt 13 - 20 *Mesure 13 - 20* **Bar 13 - 20**

Takt 25 - 34 *Mesure 25 - 34* **Bar 25 - 34**

Takt 13 - 20 *Mesure 13 - 20* **Bar 13 - 20**

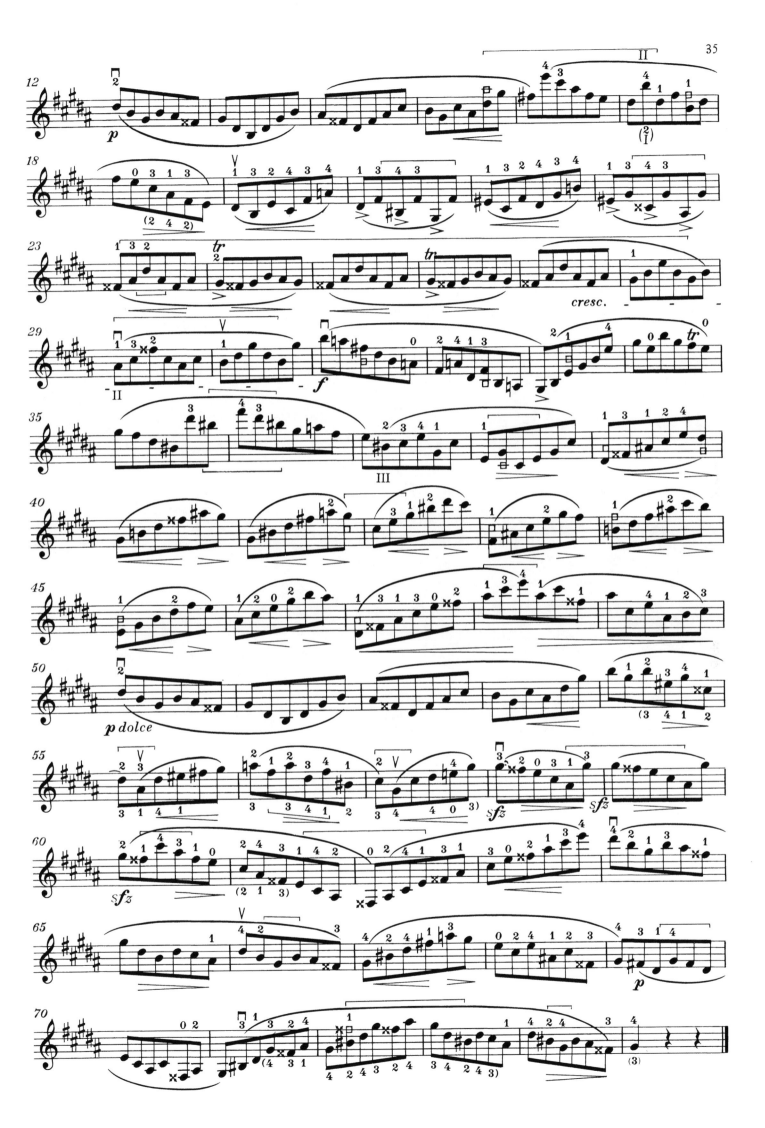

13.

Ges-Dur
G♭-major
Sol♭-majeur

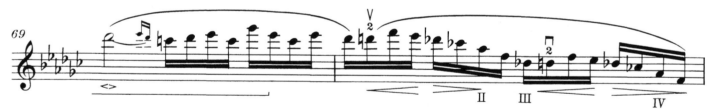

Appassionato (♩. = 60)

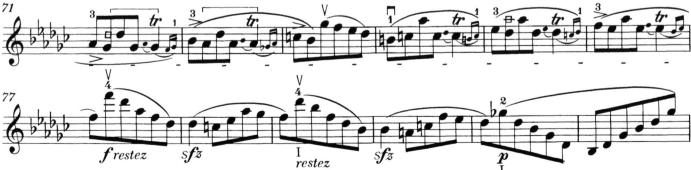

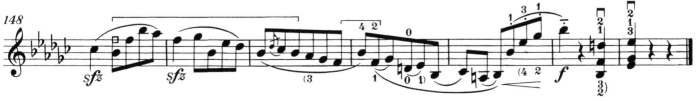

41

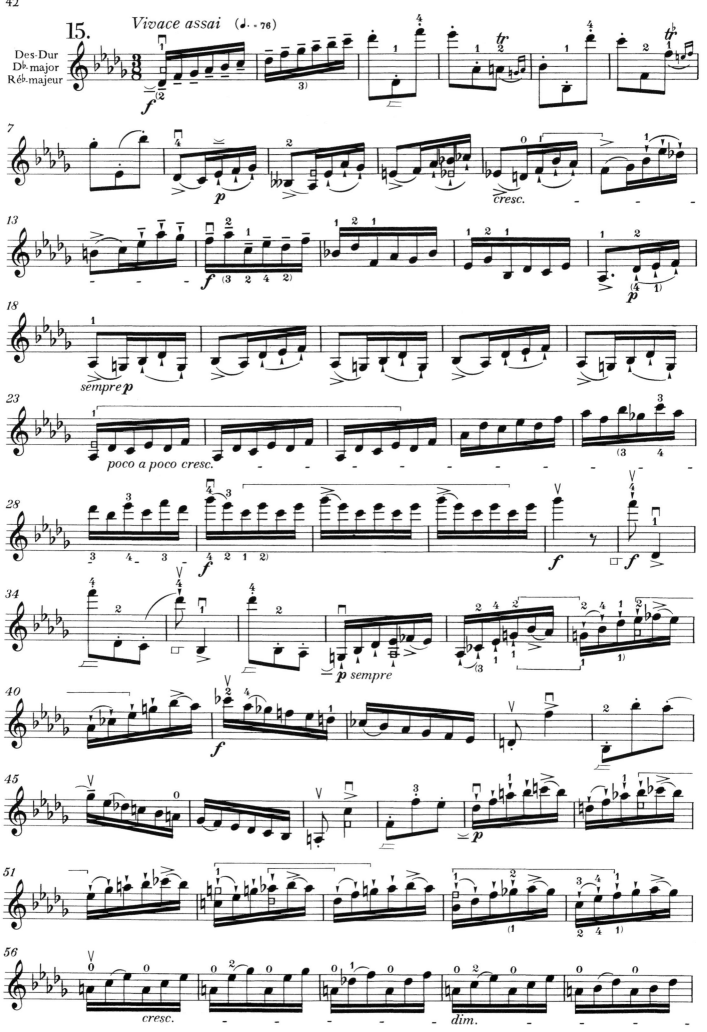

44

16.

B-Moll
Bb-minor
Sib-mineur

Andante (♪ = 104)

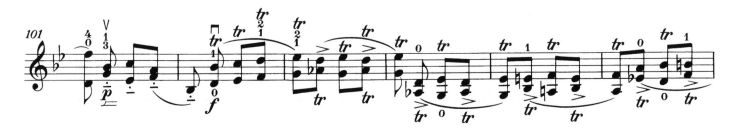

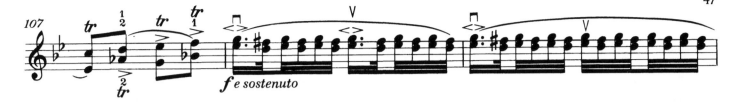

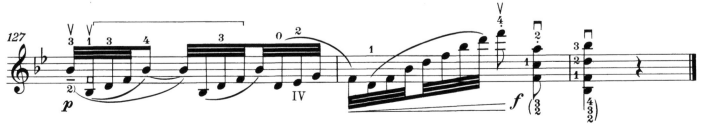

56

21. *Tempo giusto* (♩= 152)

B-Dur
B♭-major
Si♭-majeur

23.

Moderato (♩ = 100)

f sostenuto

a)

INTRODUCTION

24.

(♪ = 112)

D-Moll
D-minor
Ré-mineur

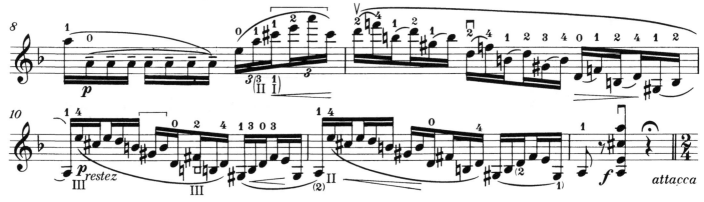

Agitato, con fuoco (♩ = 126)